Surviving Hurricanes

Elizabeth Raum

www.raintreepublishers.co.uk
Visit our website to find out
more information about
Raintree books.

To order:
☎ Phone 0845 6044371
▤ Fax +44 (0) 1865 312263
⌨ Email myorders@raintreepublishers.co.uk

Customers from outside the UK please telephone +44 1865 312262

Raintree is an imprint of **Capstone Global Library Limited**,
a company incorporated in England and Wales having its
registered office at 7 Pilgrim Street, London, EC4V 6LB –
Registered company number: 6695582

Text © Capstone Global Library Limited 2011
First published in hardback in 2011
First published in paperback in 2012
The moral rights of the proprietor have been asserted.

Edited by Louise Galpine and Laura Knowles
Designed by Victoria Allen
Original illustrations © Capstone Global Library Limited 2011
Illustrated by HLSTUDIOS
Picture research by Ruth Blair
Originated by Capstone Global Library Limited
Printed and bound in China by CTPS

ISBN 978 1 406 22216 6 (hardback)
15 14 13 12 11
10 9 8 7 6 5 4 3 2 1

ISBN 978 1 406 22223 4 (paperback)
16 15 14 13 12
10 9 8 7 6 5 4 3 2 1

British Library Cataloguing in Publication Data
Raum, Elizabeth.
Surviving hurricanes. -- (Children's true stories. Natural
disasters)
363.3'4922-dc22
A full catalogue record for this book is available from the
British Library.

Acknowledgements
We would like to thank the following for permission
to reproduce photographs: © Antony Haywood p. **15**;
Alamy p. **18** (© Danita Delimont); © Corbis p. **11**; Corbis
pp. **4** (© Daniel LeClair/Reuters), **13** (© Bettmann), **14**
(© Bettmann), **17** (© Smiley N. Pool/Dallas Morning News),
19 (© Lee Celano/Reuters), **20** (© Jerry McCrea/Star Ledger),
21 (© Michael Macor/San Francisco Chronicle), **23** (© Abir
Abdullah/epa), **24** (© Abir Abdullah/epa), **25** (© Rafiqur
Rahman/Reuters); Library of Congress pp. **7**, **8** (M.H. Zahner),
9 (C.H. Graves), **10**; © NOAA p. **27**; Shutterstock p. **26**
(© Jayne Chapman).

Cover photograph of residents of Cangnan county braving
strong winds and heavy rain brought by Typhoon Haitang in
Cangnan county in east China's Zhejiang province, reproduced
with permission of Corbis/© China Newsphoto/Reuters.

Lamia's story on page 22 is from ActionAid, www.actionaid.
org.uk/doc_lib/lamia_climate_heroine.pdf.

The author would like to thank Antony Haywood and
Christopher Nungesser for so generously sharing their stories.

We would like to thank Daniel Block for his invaluable help in
the preparation of this book.

Contents

DAILY LIFE

Read here to learn about what life was like for the children in these stories, and the impact the disaster had at home and school.

NUMBER CRUNCHING

Find out here the details about natural disasters and the damage they cause.

Survivors' lives

Read these boxes to find out what happened to the children in this book when they grew up.

HELPING HAND

Find out how people and organizations have helped to save lives.

On the scene

Read eyewitness accounts of the natural disasters in the survivors' own words.

Some words are printed in bold, **like this**. You can find out what they mean by looking in the glossary on page 30.

Introduction

Hurricanes are the biggest storms on Earth. Some hurricanes are 800 kilometres (500 miles) across.

A hurricane is a strong tropical storm. Tropical storms form over warm ocean waters near the **equator**. As the water **evaporates**, it quickly rises and releases energy. Other air moves in at great speed to take the place of the rising air, creating a strong wind. As the wind circles it draws more and more moisture from the ocean's surface. When the storm crosses cold water or land, it loses power and fades away. However, if the storm remains over warm water, it becomes larger and more powerful. When the winds reach speeds of 120 kilometres (74 miles) per hour, the storm is called a **tropical cyclone**.

Hurricane Emily slammed the Mexican coast in 2005.

Hurricane, typhoon, or cyclone?

The term tropical cyclone is used worldwide. People in the United States and Europe call these storms hurricanes. In Asia and Australia, the term typhoon or cyclone is used.

Hurricanes are frightening. Children who have lived through hurricanes always remember their fear of the storm and their relief at surviving it.

NUMBER CRUNCHING

This is the Saffir–Simpson Hurricane Wind Scale. It is based on wind speed, which is measured in kilometres or miles per hour.

Intensity of hurricane	Wind speed	Damage that may occur:
Category 1	119–152 kmph (74–95 mph)	Tree branches down; unanchored mobile homes damaged; some coastal flooding
Category 2	154–177 kmph (96–110 mph)	Mobile homes and poorly constructed buildings destroyed; small trees down; damage to piers and small boats
Category 3	178–209 kmph (111–130 mph)	Small buildings destroyed; small trees down; some inland flooding; damage to piers, docks, and boats
Category 4	211–249 kmph (131–155 mph)	Outer walls, doors, and windows severely damaged; roofs and small buildings destroyed; trees down; erosion of beaches; inland flooding
Category 5	Over 249 kmph (Over 155 mph)	Many roofs and some buildings destroyed; severe window and door damage; major flooding with water on lower floors of buildings; many people must be **evacuated**

Galveston, Texas, USA: 1900

Sarah Littlejohn, who was aged eight in 1900, lived in Galveston, Texas, USA. Galveston sits on an island in the Gulf of Mexico, about 3.2 kilometres (2 miles) off the coast of Texas. The summer of 1900 had been one of the hottest on record. Finally, on Saturday 8 September, a cool breeze began to blow.

Sarah spent that Saturday morning playing with her friend, Minnie Borden. At midday, Minnie went home, and Sarah's father returned from work. He had news. He had spoken with the local **meteorologist**, who was **predicting** a hurricane. Like most people in Galveston, Sarah's family would stay at home and wait for the storm to pass. There was no safe place to go.

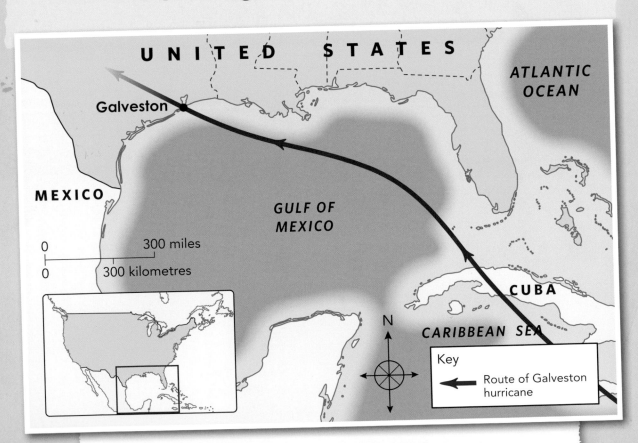

The hurricane that hit Galveston crossed over Cuba on its way west.

DAILY LIFE

In 1900, meteorologists watched the sky and the ocean for clues about the weather. They measured air temperature, wind speeds, and **air pressure**. High temperatures, high wind speeds, and low pressures may indicate that a powerful storm is on the way. Today, meteorologists also depend on **radar** and satellite pictures of storm systems. Weather predicting has improved since 1900.

The huge floods that can accompany hurricanes were strong enough to force houses from their foundations.

A scream in the night

The tide was high. Waves crashed against the shore. Soon, water filled the streets of Galveston. Strong winds blew shutters off houses, carried away sheds, and sent tree branches flying. Sarah's father helped neighbours to nail windows and doors shut.

By 6.00 p.m. that evening, water covered the ground floor of Sarah's house. When everyone went upstairs, they found that the roof was leaking and the beds were wet. They crowded into the bathroom to stay dry. Sarah heard someone scream. She later wrote, "The sounds we heard that night were just dreadful."

Children had nowhere to go after the Galveston hurricane. This boy is playing around in **debris** left by the disaster.

Destruction all around

When her mother looked out of the window, she saw something large and white float by. It was the cottage next door. Before the night was over, thousands of homes were destroyed. Sarah's family and their house survived the storm.

On the scene

The **storm surge** destroyed everything between Sarah's house and the beach. She wrote, "The water went down very rapidly, and soon it was daylight Sunday morning. We looked out of the window, and of all the beautiful houses between our house and the beach, not one was left."

In the chaos after the storm, many people did not know where help would come from. Here, supply wagons are delivering much needed food supplies.

Disaster

The Galveston Hurricane is the worst natural disaster in United States history. More than 6,000 people drowned or were killed by flying debris. The Category 4 hurricane destroyed 3,636 houses. For the survivors, there was no clean water to drink and very little food. The Red Cross and other relief groups rushed to help.

Rebuilding

When the people of Galveston rebuilt their city, they built a **seawall** to protect against high waves. **Engineers** began to raise the level of the city by 5 metres (17 feet) at the seawall to prevent flooding. It was a huge job, but it helped protect Galveston from future disasters.

In 1904, a man stands on top of a portion of Galveston's new seawall.

On the scene

Clara Barton wrote letters to the US government from Galveston about the flood. On 18 September 1900, she wrote, "There seems to be an unusually large number of children with no one to care for them or who knows them. We will help them as far as possible, gather them in, and the world will give them homes."

Clara Barton was head of the American Red Cross in 1900.

HELPING HAND

New York City children raised $27,907 (over $712,000 in today's dollars, and roughly £454,000) to help the children of Galveston.

Darwin, Australia: 1974

On 24 December 1974, eight-year-old Antony Haywood went to bed dreaming about Christmas presents. He didn't know that a hurricane was headed for his hometown of Darwin, Australia. The storm had formed in the Arafura Sea, northeast of Darwin. As meteorologists at the Tropical Cyclone Warning Centre watched, the storm slowed and seemed to be turning away. Then it looped back towards Darwin.

N

Arafura Sea

Darwin

A U S T R A L I A

Key
— Route of tropical low
— Route of Tropical Cyclone Tracy

0   100 miles

0   100 kilometres

Darwin is on the coast of Australia's Northern Territory. This map shows the path of Cyclone Tracy.

Midnight visitor

Cyclone Tracy, a Category 5 hurricane, struck the city of Darwin at midnight. Antony's mother woke Antony and his younger brother Steve just before midnight. She rushed the boys in to her bedroom, wrapped them in blankets, and pushed them under her big bed. Then she crawled in beside them. Steve fell asleep – but not Antony. The wind howled, windows shattered, and water dripped onto his face.

Few houses remained standing after the hurricane.

HELPING HAND

Antony's mum chose wisely. The bedroom had three brick walls. Hiding beneath the big bed offered protection against broken glass and flying debris. "I was scared," Antony said, "but mum told us we would be OK which made me feel much better."

A pile of bricks

When morning arrived, Antony, Steve, and their mum crawled out of the wreckage. They had survived, but the house was just a pile of bricks.

Antony refused to leave home. After all, it was Christmas Day. He searched for the presents that had been underneath the Christmas tree. All he found was a broken action figure for his brother, a toy gun for himself, and a blouse with flowers on it for his mum. It was all they had left.

NUMBER CRUNCHING

This chart shows the damage caused by Cyclone Tracy:

Deaths	Injuries	Ships lost at sea	Buildings destroyed	Evacuees
66	790	21	around 10,000	around 35,000

Evacuating

Cyclone Tracy destroyed Darwin. It is one of the worst natural disasters in Australia's history. Most people **evacuated**, or left Darwin immediately after the storm. Antony and his family moved in with relatives in Perth, Western Australia. People across the country provided temporary homes, supplies, and money. As the city was rebuilt, people moved back. The new buildings were built to survive hurricane winds.

Today, Antony enjoys camping with his family near Alice Springs, Australia.

Antony's life now

Today, Antony works for the electric company that helped bring power back to Darwin after the cyclone. "I love Darwin," he says. "My boys are fascinated when they see photos of Darwin after Tracy hit."

New Orleans, Louisiana, USA: 2005

On 28 August 2005, a storm in the Gulf of Mexico developed into a Category 5 hurricane. It headed towards the Louisiana and Mississippi coasts of the United States.

Chris's story

Chris Nungesser, aged 11, lived in a suburb of New Orleans. He was watching TV as a meteorologist predicted that Hurricane Katrina would hit New Orleans. "It freaked us out," Chris said. Everyone in the neighbourhood began boarding up windows and gathering emergency supplies.

Hurricane Katrina hit Louisiana, Mississippi, and Alabama.

Leaving home

People were ordered to evacuate. About 960,000 out of 1.2 million people in New Orleans left the area. Chris and his family went to New Iberia, Louisiana. Roads were jammed with traffic.

When Chris reached New Iberia, he watched TV reports of rain gushing into the streets of New Orleans. **Dykes** surrounding the city had broken, and the streets filled with water.

Stuck in the city

Not everyone could leave New Orleans. Many who stayed were too old or sick to leave. Others were poor. They had no car, and public transportation wasn't working.

Floodwaters covered the city of New Orleans.

NUMBER CRUNCHING

In total, 1,833 people died because of Hurricane Katrina. In Louisiana, almost half of those who died were over 75 years old. Many were too sick or poor to leave their homes.

Temporary homes

Some evacuees stayed in **disaster centres** or were taken in by kind strangers. Others moved into temporary trailers provided by the Federal Emergency Management Agency (FEMA). Chris and his family moved in with an aunt and uncle in Houston, Texas. He began attending a school in Houston. The other children were kind, and the teachers were sympathetic.

The Astrodome sports stadium in Houston, Texas was used as a disaster centre to house hurricane evacuees.

Returning home

Chris flew home in mid-October. "Seeing the damage from above was frightening," he said. He saw boats and houses sprawled over roads. There was plenty of work ahead for the hurricane victims.

Chris's family was lucky. Even though the ground floor of their house was damaged, it could be fixed. Sewer water had backed up in the pipes of their house. It stank.

People in Metairie, where Chris lived, used boats to travel through the flooded streets.

HELPING HAND

Talia Leman of Iowa, USA was 10 years old when Hurricane Katrina struck New Orleans. She set up a website called RandomKid.org to raise money for hurricane victims. In the first three months, children raised more than $5 million (about £3.2 million) for hurricane victims.

Total losses in New Orleans

Many people decided not to return to New Orleans. The city population dropped by 223,388 people within two years of the hurricane. About 205,000 houses were totally destroyed there.

Those who returned began repairing and rebuilding. However, many people who lived in poor neighbourhoods lacked the money or supplies they needed to rebuild. They lived in FEMA trailers for years. By June 2010, nearly five years after the hurricane, there were still 350 FEMA trailers in New Orleans.

Many kids, such as 13-year-old Haylee Gaw of Kinnelon, New Jersey, USA, helped to collect clothing and other supplies needed in New Orleans.

NUMBER CRUNCHING

More houses were lost in Hurricane Katrina than in any other natural disaster in United States history.

Beyond New Orleans

Because New Orleans is a major city, it received lots of coverage on television and in newspapers. However, Hurricane Katrina also damaged many other areas. The most damage occurred in Louisiana, Mississippi, and Alabama. Georgia, Florida, Kentucky, and Ohio suffered damage from flooding.

Aisha Turner, aged eight, lost her belongings in the hurricane. Here, she is searching through clothes at a relief centre to find an outfit to wear to school.

HELPING HAND

Volunteers came from all over the United States to help with rebuilding. The Red Cross, Salvation Army, and Habitat for Humanity were among the many organizations to offer help. People from the rest of the world helped, too. All together, 70 nations offered aid.

Bangladesh: 2007

Cyclone Sidr, a powerful Category 4 hurricane, hit Bangladesh in November 2007. Over 3,000 people died. Most people died in floods caused by the storm surge.

Lamia's story

Seven-year-old Lamia and her family live near the coast of Bangladesh, in a village called Char Bangla. When her teacher warned that a cyclone was on the way, Lamia and five friends went door-to-door warning villagers to go to the cyclone shelter. Many did. But Lamia's father refused. Lamia grabbed his hand and pulled until he agreed to take shelter. Lamia and her friends saved many lives that day.

This map shows the route of Cyclone Sidr and the low-lying land that was flooded by the storm surge.

River Ganges

INDIA

B A N G L A D E S H

INDIA

0   100 miles

0   100 kilometres

N

Key

⬅ Route of Cyclone Sidr

▨ Land flooded by storm surge

Bay of Bengal

MYANMAR

Dangerous play

Many homes and schools were damaged by the cyclone. Some children played among the debris. They searched for anything that might be useful. However, it was dangerous play. The debris included sharp items, bits of metal, and even fallen power lines.

Many houses in the villages of Bangladesh are not built out of strong materials. This woman's house was destroyed by the hurricane.

NUMBER CRUNCHING

It is thought that more than 80 per cent of those killed by Cyclone Sidr were children. They were not able to swim or escape the storm surge fast enough. Many other children were injured or lost family members.

A terrible toll

During hurricanes, high winds and floods kill people and livestock, destroy buildings, and ruin crops. As a very poor country, Bangladesh is vulnerable to natural disasters. This is because families often have poor housing and not enough money to be able to leave an area if they are at risk.

Cyclone Sidr caused serious food and water shortages. In the weeks after the cyclone, people became ill by drinking unclean water. Others suffered from snakebites as they waded through floodwaters.

People waited for deliveries of clean water and food after the cyclone.

HELPING HAND

By June 2008, Save the Children had provided food to 176,000 families, medicine for 80,000 people, and provided safe play areas for 20,000 children.

Rebuilding

Relief groups such as UNICEF and Save the Children brought water, food, and basic supplies such as cooking pots, matches, and soap. Plastic sheets helped protect hurricane victims from the rain. Many other groups and countries offered aid. Repairing the damage from Cyclone Sidr will take years.

In December 2007, pop singer Shakira visited Bangladesh as a Goodwill Ambassador for UNICEF. She met children affected by Cyclone Sidr.

NUMBER CRUNCHING

Since 1980, more than 600,000 people in Bangladesh have died in tropical cyclones, most from drowning. The chart below shows the terrible losses caused by Cyclone Sidr throughout Bangladesh:

People killed	3,033
People injured	34,511
People missing	1,828
Farm animals killed	462,815
Houses destroyed	363,346
Houses damaged	815,628
Schools affected	9,202

Conclusion

There is no way to stop hurricanes. But we can reduce the damage they cause. In Galveston, USA, building a seawall and raising the level of the land protected the city. In Darwin, Australia, people built stronger houses to withstand hurricane winds. Today, scientists are looking for new solutions to save lives, buildings, and belongings.

Preserving wetlands

Preserving natural **wetlands** will help reduce hurricane damage to the US Gulf coast. Wetlands can reduce flooding and protect shorelines. They act as sponges, storing water from heavy rains and storm surges.

Coastal wetlands such as this one in Louisiana, USA help absorb storm surges.

Weather planes fly into the eye of hurricanes to gather information needed to predict when and where a hurricane will strike. Warning people about a hurricane can save lives.

Better building materials

In Bangladesh, engineers are developing new building materials. One idea is to mix **jute**, a common plant there, with plastic. Houses made of this material would bend, but not break, in hurricane winds. They would float on the storm surge, keeping people safe inside until danger has passed.

Krista Villarreal's life

When Krista Villarreal was seven years-old, her Texas school was evacuated because of flooding from Hurricane Norma in 1981. "I was carried out – that makes quite an impression on a 2nd grader [Year 3 pupil]. I was fascinated by weather." Her fascination continued. Today, Krista is a meteorologist.

Mapping hurricanes

Hurricanes, which form in tropical waters, always strike coastal areas first. They grow weaker as they cross over land.

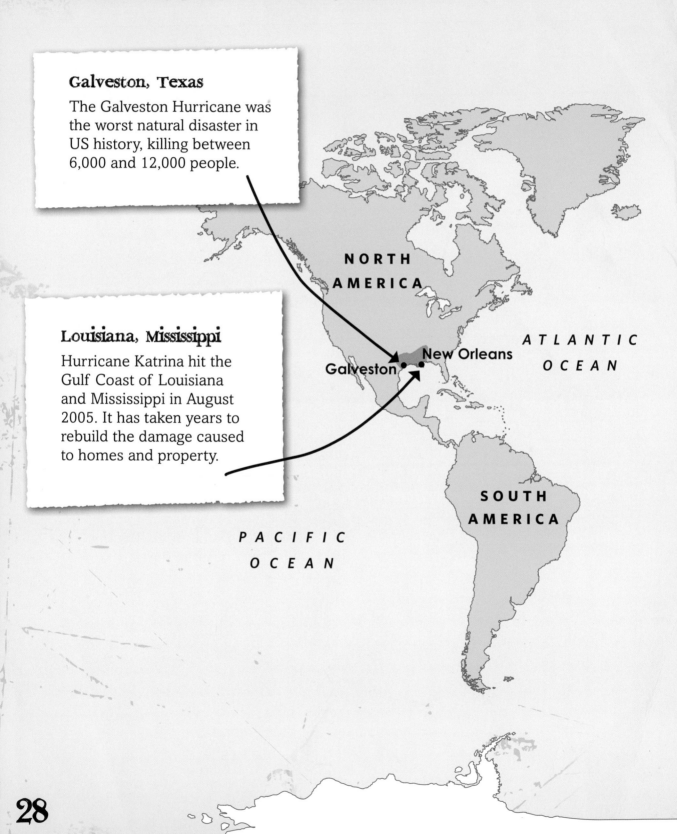

Galveston, Texas

The Galveston Hurricane was the worst natural disaster in US history, killing between 6,000 and 12,000 people.

Louisiana, Mississippi

Hurricane Katrina hit the Gulf Coast of Louisiana and Mississippi in August 2005. It has taken years to rebuild the damage caused to homes and property.

NORTH AMERICA

ATLANTIC OCEAN

New Orleans

Galveston

SOUTH AMERICA

PACIFIC OCEAN

Bangladesh

Bangladesh suffers hurricanes, floods, and tornadoes. Almost all of Bangladesh lies only just above **sea level**. Most of its people are poor.

EUROPE

ASIA

Bangladesh

AFRICA

PACIFIC OCEAN

INDIAN OCEAN

Darwin **AUSTRALASIA**

Darwin, Australia

In 1974, Cyclone Tracy destroyed the city of Darwin, Australia.

ANTARCTICA

Glossary

air pressure weight of air pressing down on the earth. A change in air pressure indicates a change in the weather.

debris remains of things broken or destroyed; litter; rubbish

disaster centre protected area to sit out a natural disaster

dyke bank built to control or hold back the water of the sea or a river

engineer person who constructs or manages building projects

equator imaginary circle around the earth that is equally distant from the North Pole and South Pole

evacuate leave an area for reasons of safety

evacuee person who leaves an area for reasons of safety

evaporate give off moisture

jute strong, coarse fibre from a plant that grows in Asia. It is often used for making sacks.

meteorologist person who studies the science behind the weather

predict say that something will happen in the future, usually based on research or other information

radar way of detecting distant objects and determining their speed and position by turning radio waves into images. Radar is used on weather maps.

sea level level of the ocean's surface

seawall strong wall designed to prevent flooding from the sea

storm surge seawater pushed onto land by hurricane winds

tropical cyclone massive storm that develops over warm ocean waters

wetlands land that has a wet and spongy soil, such as a marsh, swamp, or bog

Find out more

Books

How Does a Cloud Become a Thunderstorm? (How Does It Happen?),
Mike Graf (Raintree, 2010)

Howling Hurricanes (Awesome Forces of Nature), Louise and Richard
Spilsbury (Raintree, 2010)

Hurricane (Wild Weather), Catherine Chambers (Heinemann Library, 2008)

Websites

eo.ucar.edu/webweather/hurricanehome.html
This is a fun website for children to learn about extreme weather, including
games to play and activities to do.

skydiary.com/kids/hurricanes.html
Visit this website to find out information about hurricanes and how
they are formed.

www.fema.gov/kids/hurr.htm
This website tells children what to do in the event of a hurricane.

www.nhm.ac.uk/nature-online/earth/volcanoes-earthquakes
Visit the Natural History Museum website to find out all about hurrianes
and other natural disasters.

www.randomkid.org
Set up by Talia Leman, this website provides support for those children
who have been involved in a natural disaster as well as providing ways
for children to help others who have suffered.

Index